PUZZLE IT OUT!

COUNTING
PUZZLES

BY PAUL VIRR AND LISA REGAN
ILLUSTRATED BY AMANDA ENRIGHT

WINDMILL
BOOKS

Published in 2020 by Windmill Books,
an Imprint of Rosen Publishing
29 East 21st Street, New York, NY 10010

Cataloging-in-Publication Data
Names: Virr, Paul. | Regan, Lisa.
Title: Counting puzzles / Paul Virr and Lisa Regan.
Description: New York : Windmill Books, 2020. | Series: Puzzle it out! | Includes glossary and index.
Identifiers: ISBN 9781538392003 (pbk.) | ISBN 9781538392027 (library bound) | ISBN 9781538392010 (6 pack)
Subjects: LCSH: Mathematical recreations--Juvenile literature. | Counting--Juvenile literature. | Logic puzzles--Juvenile literature.
Classification: LCC QA95.V577 2019 | DDC 793.74--dc23

Manufactured in the United States of America

CPSIA Compliance Information: Batch BS19WM: For Further Information contact Rosen Publishing, New York, New York at 1-800-237-9932

CONTENTS

Counting Sheep

Little Bo Peep is counting her sheep! How many black sheep are there? How many white sheep? And how many sheep are there altogether?

Sharing Snacks

These children like to share. Can you give each child the same number of strawberries?

Gone Fishing

Who has caught the most fish, the red team or the blue team? How many more fish did they catch than the losing team?

VEGETABLE PATCH

Flowers and vegetables are everywhere!
How many groups can you see that include five
of the same vegetable or flower together?

Honey Hive

Who has made the most honey—the bees with the red, orange, or yellow honey?

FLOWER FAIRIES

Maisy the fairy is looking for purple flowers.
Her friend Daisy is looking for white ones.
Who will find the most flowers?

Cupcakes to Go!

Time for a tasty treat! If each child buys a different cupcake, which plate will have three cupcakes left?

a

b

c

d

DOWN ON THE FARM

How many animals can you see on the farm?
How many would be left if all the sheep ran away?

Flower Finder

Just look at all these pretty flowers! How many flowers can you find that have six petals?

Pirate Treasure!

Use your finger to follow the arrows on the map to find Captain Redbeard's treasure. The numbers show you how many squares to move in each direction.

START
3 →

2 →

1 ↓

1 ←

2 ↓

1 ←

2 →

2 ↑

2 ↓

Blowing Bubbles

Bubbles, bubbles everywhere!
How many groups of three can you spot?

Fishy Fun

These happy fish are playing under the sea.
How many red fish are there?
And how many blue fish?

How many orange-and-white fish can you see?

Wacky Wheels

Everyone is whizzing around! How many wheels can you count? How many wheels would be left if all the scooters zoomed off home?

Moon Walk

Ready for blastoff? Use your finger to follow the arrows to reach your rocket safely. The numbers tell you how many squares to move in each direction.

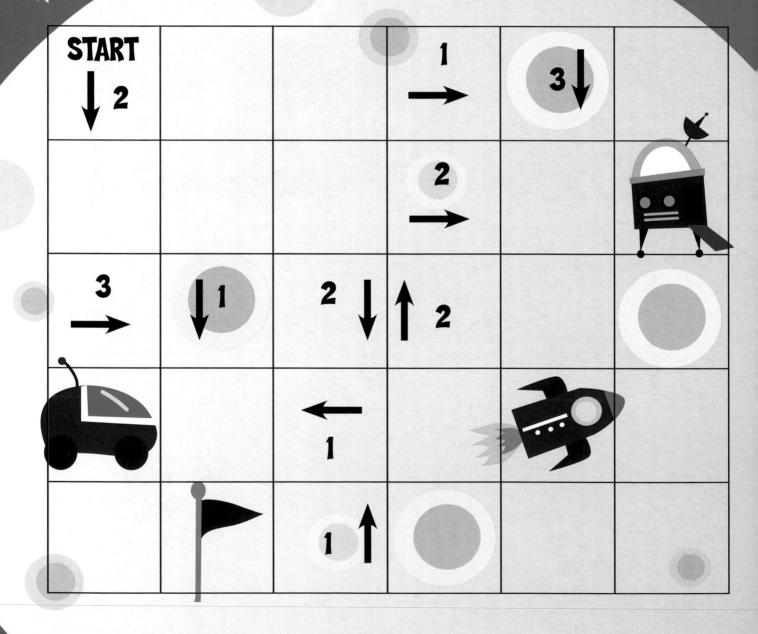

Round Town

There are so many circles in Round Town!
But how many wheels can you see?

SAFARI SPECTACLE

How many wild animals can you see?
How many would be left if
all the zebras ran away?

LOOPY LOOPS

Which toy plane has looped the loop the most times?

Crazy Castles

These children are drawing pictures of castles. Which castle contains the most square blocks?

Costume Party

Let's dress up! What shape appears most on the costumes at this fun fashion show?

Ice Cream!

Do more animals like chocolate or strawberry ice cream?
How many ice cream cones are there altogether?

TREAT TIME

It's treat time for these children. How many candy canes has Mr. Candy sold? And how many lollipops?

ANSWERS

Page 4 Counting Sheep

There are 4 black sheep and 3 white sheep.
There are 7 sheep altogether.

Page 5 Sharing Snacks

Each child should have 3 strawberries.

Page 6 Gone Fishing

The red team has caught 11 fish, and the blue team
has caught 7 fish. The red team has caught 4 more
fish than the blue team.

Page 7 Vegetable Patch

There are 2 groups of
5 flowers and vegetables.

Page 8 Honey Hive

The yellow bees have made the most honey.

Page 9 Flower Fairies

There are 19 white flowers and 8 purple
ones, so Daisy will find the most.

Page 10 Cupcakes to Go!

Plate b.

Page 11 Down on the Farm

There are 16 animals on the farm. If all the sheep ran away, there would be 11 animals left.

Pages 12-13 Flower Finder

There are 6 flowers with 6 petals.

Page 14 Pirate Treasure!

Page 15 Blowing Bubbles

There are 5 groups of 3 bubbles.

Page 16 Fishy Fun

There are 3 red fish, and 5 blue fish.
There are 7 orange-and-white fish.

Page 17 Wacky Wheels

There are 18 wheels in the picture.
There would be 8 wheels left if the
scooters zoomed home.

Page 18 Moon Walk

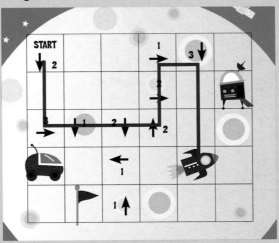

Page 19 Round Town

There are 8 wheels in the picture.

Page 20-21 Safari Spectacle

There are 14 wild animals altogether.
If all the zebras ran away, there would be 11 left.

Page 22 Loopy Loops

Plane e.

Page 23 Crazy Castles

The orange castle.

Pages 24–25 Costume Party

Triangles.

Page 26 Ice Cream!

More animals like chocolate
ice cream than strawberry.

Page 27 Treat Time

Mr. Candy has sold 4 candy canes,
and 7 lollipops.

GLOSSARY

costumes Clothes for dressing up.

hive A bee's nest, or home.

Little Bo Peep A character in a nursery rhyme who loses her sheep.

loop the loop To perform a loop in an airplane.

petals The colorful parts of a flower.

scooter A foot-operated vehicle with two wheels.

INDEX